THE
LIPIZZANER
HORSE

by Charlotte Wilcox

Reading Consultant:
Sandy Heaberlin
Lipizzan Association of North America

C A P S T O N E P R E S S
M A N K A T O , M I N N E S O T A

C A P S T O N E   P R E S S

818 North Willow Street • Mankato, Minnesota 56001

Printed in the United States of America.

Library of Congress Cataloging-in-Publication Data
Wilcox, Charlotte.
   The Lipizzaner horse/by Charlotte Wilcox
   p. cm.--(Learning about horses)
   Includes bibliographical references (p. 45) and index.
   Summary: Presents the history, physical characteristics, and the abilities
   of the Lipizzaner horse.
   ISBN 1-56065-464-3
   1. Lipizzaner horse--Juvenile literature. [1. Lipizzaner horse.]
I. Title. II. Series.
SF293.L5W54   1997
636.1'3--dc20

                                        96-42318
                                          CIP
                                           AC

Photo credits
Brian Beck, cover, 30, 41, 42
Dan Polin, 6, 14, 28, 36
Jim Rowan, 8
FPG, 10, 18, 26, 32
Betty Crowell, 12
Julie Green, 25, 38-39
Lipizzan Association of North America, 17, 20, 34

Table of Contents

Quick Facts about the Lipizzaner Horse

Description

Height:	Lipizzaners stand 14-1/2 to 15-3/4 hands from the ground to the top of the shoulders. That is between 58 and 63 inches (147 and 160 centimeters) tall.
Weight:	A full-grown Lipizzaner weighs about 1,000 pounds (450 kilograms).
Physical features:	Lipizzaners have muscular bodies, arched necks, and long manes and tails. They are very athletic.
Colors:	At birth, Lipizzaners are brown, black, or dark gray. As they grow, they get more white hairs. They turn all white when they are between six and 10 years old.

Development

History of breed:	Lipizzaners are descended from Spanish horses bred by the royal family of Austria.
Place of origin:	They came from parts of what is now Austria, Italy, and Slovenia.
Numbers:	There are about 2,500 Lipizzaner horses in the world. About 800 of them live in North America.

Life History

Life span:	Lipizzaners can live to be 30 to 35 years old. This is a long life for a horse.

Uses

The Lipizzaner horse is famous for its ability to perform a style of riding called dressage (dreh-SAHJ). The horse performs complicated movements on command from the rider. Lipizzaners also pull carriages and march in parades.

Chapter 1

The Dancing White Horses

Some people say riding on a Lipizzaner horse is like floating on a cloud. Lipizzaners are powerful and graceful. Lipizzaner horses can perform movements that other horses cannot. They learn very special skills.

Today, the most famous Lipizzaners perform in shows. Show Lipizzaners are male horses called stallions. They prance to music and do amazing steps and difficult movements. For centuries, you could only see them in a few places in Europe. Now, they perform all around the world.

Some say riding on a Lipizzaner is like floating on a cloud.

Lipizzaners are very special horses because there are not many of them. The Lipizzaner breed started about 400 years ago in Austria. Even now, most Lipizzaners still live in that area of Europe. There are about 2,500 Lipizzaners in the world.

Many people fell in love with Lipizzaners after Disney made a movie about them in 1963. It was called *The Miracle of the White Stallions*.

Today, there are about 2,500 Lipizzaners in the world.

Chapter 2

The Beginnings of the Lipizzaner

In 1562, the emperor of Austria was looking for good horses. He found them in Spain. The Spanish horses were fast. They were strong enough to carry a soldier in heavy armor. They could jump high. They could make quick turns in small places.

The emperor bought some of these Spanish stallions and female horses called mares. He started breeding them at his farm at Kladrub, Austria. Ten years later, the emperor started a riding school. He hired the finest horsemen in his kingdom to teach at the school. They used the emperor's best Spanish horses. The school was called the Spanish Riding School.

The Spanish Riding School trains horses and their handlers.

The riding school taught the complicated movements that Lipizzaners still do today.

At the school, young Austrian men learned how to handle horses. They learned special parade drills. They also learned how to fight on horseback. They used the style of riding called dressage. In this style, the horse performs complicated movements on command from the rider.

Spanish Horses at Lipizza

The emperor's brother bought 33 Spanish horses in 1580. He took them to a farm near Lipizza. This town was a part of Austria for many years. It is now part of Slovenia and is spelled Lipica.

The Austrian royal family raised Spanish horses on their farms for 350 years. Breeders at the Kladrub farm crossed the Spanish horses with heavier breeds. They developed a line of top carriage horses.

At Lipizza, the Spanish horses were crossed with Arabian, Italian, and local horses. This produced a lighter, more athletic horse. These horses were perfectly suited for dressage.

Over the years, the horses adapted to their surroundings to survive.

The land around Lipizza is rocky limestone. This helped the horses develop strong hooves and bones. Lipizza also has a harsh climate. This produced a hardy horse. Lipizzaners mature slowly but live a long life.

The horses from Lipizza became favorites of the Austrian army and the royal family. People began calling them Lipizzaners. Sometimes, the name is shortened to Lipizzan.

At first, only the Austrian military and noble families could own Lipizzaners. The stallions carried men into battle. The mares pulled carriages.

Horses at War

During the 1700s and 1800s, Lipizzaner stallions became great war horses. They could perform complicated movements to save their riders' lives during battle. Trainers at the Spanish Riding School were good at teaching horses these new steps and special movements.

When a rider was attacked, his stallion would leap into the air over the heads of the enemies. Some stallions learned to strike out with their hooves from midair. This frightened enemy soldiers.

The Lipizzaner war horses became the envy of other armies. The Austrians guarded them carefully. They had to keep the Lipizzaners away from enemy armies. The horses' lives were in danger.

The first threat came in 1781. To escape from the French army, 300 Lipizzaners made a 40-day march to Hungary. They were kept there until it

Today's Lipizzaners still perform the war movements that would save their riders' lives during battle.

was safe to return to Lipizza. The horses were moved several times between 1805 and 1815 to escape capture.

There were many wars in Europe in the early 1800s. Many kings were killed in revolutions. Their families could no longer keep expensive horses and riding schools. But in Austria, the Spanish Riding School kept on teaching horsemanship and dressage. If it were not for this school, these ancient arts of handling and caring for horses might have been lost.

World War I

In 1915, Austria was fighting World War I (1914-1918). The royal family saw that the Lipizzaner herd was in danger. They decided to split up the herd. If enemies captured the horses at one place, others would be saved somewhere else. Some of the mares and breeding stallions went to a farm near Vienna. The young horses, called foals, went to Kladrub. A third group of breeding stock stayed at Lipizza.

Four years later, Austria lost World War I. The royal family lost their power. Czechoslovakia took over the farm at Kladrub with its Lipizzaner

The Spanish Riding School kept alive the art of handling and caring for horses.

horses. Italy took over the region around Lipizza. The farm where part of the Lipizzaner herd lived now belonged to Italy.

But the peace plan allowed the Austrian government to keep half of the horses at Lipizza. In 1920, these horses went to a new home at Piber, Austria. Piber became their permanent home.

Chapter 3

The Great Horse Rescue

In the 1940s, Austria was at war again. This time it was World War II (1939-1945). It was the worst fighting Europe had ever seen. The Lipizzaners were in danger from bombs.

Colonel Alois Podhajsky (Poh-JHAH-skee) was the director of the Spanish Riding School. He was one of the greatest horsemen of the 20th century. He took quick action to save his stallions' lives. He put them on a train and sent them 200 miles (320 kilometers) away to a friend's farm.

The journey was hard for the stallions. There was barely enough food for the trip.

The Lipizzaners' permanent home was in Piber, Austria.

General George S. Patton (left), teamed up with Colonel Alois Podhajsky to save the Lipizzaner breed.

Bombs and gunfire roared. Starving homeless people tried to steal the horses for meat.

Finally, Podhajsky and the stallions reached their destination. But bad news was waiting for them. The United States Army was in the area. The United States fought against Austria in World War II.

Two Old Friends

News of the famous stallions soon reached General George S. Patton. He was commander of the U.S. forces in the area. General Patton was a great horseman himself. He was an old friend of Podhajsky's. In their younger days, the two men had both competed on horseback in the Olympic Games.

Patton immediately went to visit his friend. The general fell in love with the white stallions. He promised to put them under the protection of the U.S. Army.

The school stallions were finally safe. But the mares, foals, and breeding stallions from Piber were still in danger. If they were lost, there would be no more foals to carry on the Lipizzaner breed.

Still in Danger

During World War II, the Austrian government was under the control of Germany. The Germans loved the Lipizzaner horses, too. Because of the heavy bombing around Piber,

the Germans moved the Lipizzaners to an army post at Hostau. This was in what is now the Czech Republic.

But the Lipizzaners were not safe at Hostau. The Russian army was at war with Germany. The Russians were closing in on Hostau. If a battle broke out, the horses could be killed. Or the Russians might use them for meat.

Enemies Work Together

Once again, friendship between two enemies saved the horses. On April 26, 1945, U.S. soldiers captured a German general near Hostau. The U.S. officer in command was Colonel Charles H. Reed. He did not lock up the German general. Instead, he invited him to dinner. The two officers became friends.

The German general showed Reed pictures of the Lipizzaner horses. He said U.S. and Canadian prisoners of war were taking care of the horses at Hostau.

Reed knew the Russians would arrive soon. He immediately telephoned General Patton. Patton gave orders to attack Hostau and rescue the prisoners and horses.

But there were problems with this plan. The German soldiers at Hostau would fight back. If a gun battle broke out, the horses might be shot and killed.

Attacking Hostau

Once again, Colonel Reed used his ability to make friends with his enemies. He convinced the German officers in the area that Hostau should surrender to the United States. Reed promised to treat the German soldiers fairly. He promised not to let the Russians capture the prized horses. The Germans agreed to the plan.

To save the Germans' honor, Reed still had to attack Hostau. He fired a few shots at the post. That way, it did not look like the Germans were giving up for no reason.

The Germans quickly surrendered to the U.S. troops. They were glad they would not have to face the Russians. They were glad the Russians would not get the Lipizzaners. A German honor guard saluted the U.S. troops as they entered the post.

Colonel Reed spent the rest of the day inspecting the horses. A week later, the war ended. Colonel Podhajsky flew to Hostau to care for the Lipizzaners. But the horses were not out of danger yet.

Germany and Austria lost the war. Russia was in control of the area around Hostau. The Russian and Czech governments both expected to keep the horses at Hostau. But the United States quickly took action. The U.S. Army secretly moved the whole herd out of danger.

Today's Lipizzaners have never seen a war.

Safe at Home

Colonel Podhajsky and his stallions returned to Vienna in 1955. The mares, foals, and breeding stallions returned to the farm at Piber. Today, they still enjoy a peaceful life there.

The Piber farm and the Spanish Riding School are still owned by the Austrian government. Today, anyone can own a Lipizzaner horse. Visitors to Vienna still come to watch the stallions perform their amazing war movements. But today's Lipizzaners have never seen a war.

Chapter 4

The Lipizzaner Today

A famous opera singer brought the first Lipizzaners to North America in 1937. Her name was Countess Maria Jeritza. The horses were a gift from the Austrian government. The U.S. Army brought three more Lipizzaner stallions and six mares to North America after their rescue in 1945.

Other people brought a few Lipizzaners to North America in the 1950s and 1960s. Lipizzaners are still rare today. There are only about 800 in the United States, and a handful in Canada and Mexico.

Lipizzaner Associations

The Lipizzan Association of North America keeps track of the Lipizzaner horses born in the United

Countess Maria Jeritza brought the first Lipizzaners to North America in 1937.

States, Canada, and Mexico. They keep pedigrees of the horses. A pedigree is a horse's family tree. The Lipizzan Association of North America sends the pedigrees to the Lipizzan International Federation in Europe. This group keeps track of all the Lipizzaners in the world.

To be registered with the Lipizzan International Federation, a Lipizzaner must be purebred. The registries also keep track of horses that are at least half Lipizzaner.

What Lipizzaners Look Like

Lipizzaners are considered to be among the most beautiful horses in the world. One reason is the proud way they hold their head and body. They have long, flowing manes and tails. Their eyes are large and friendly.

Lipizzaners are powerful horses. They have muscular shoulders and hindquarters. They also have a strong, arched neck. When fully grown, they weigh about 1,000 pounds (450 kilograms).

Lipizzaners are powerful horses. They have muscular shoulders and hindquarters.

Lipizzaners are not very tall horses. A horse's height is measured from the ground to the withers. The withers are the spot at the top of the horse's shoulders. Most Lipizzaners stand between 14-1/2 and 15-3/4 hands. One hand equals four inches (10 centimeters).

Lipizzaner foals are brown, black, or dark gray when they are born. They get more and more white hairs as they grow older. Most Lipizzaners are all white by the time they are six to 10 years old.

Once in a while, a dark-colored Lipizzaner is born. The darks do not turn white. Dark Lipizzaners are seldom used for breeding in Austria.

Even so, the Spanish Riding School always uses one dark stallion in its shows. It is a tradition. All the other horses in the show are white.

It is a tradition to use one dark stallion in every show.

Chapter 5

The Spanish Riding School

The Spanish Riding School is the oldest riding school in the world. Thousands of people come to watch the public performances. The shows are held at the Winter Riding Hall in Vienna.

It took six years to build this beautiful arena. It was started in 1729 and was finished in 1735. Large, fancy light fixtures made of crystal hang from the high ceiling. The balconies have gold and ivory decorations.

This school has very high standards of horsemanship. Only the most dedicated trainers and riders work at the school. They use only the most talented Lipizzaner stallions.

It took six years to build the beautiful Winter Riding Hall.

It takes many years to train a Lipizzaner.

Learning to Ride

At the Spanish Riding School, horses and riders train each other. Experienced riders take the young horses through their first paces. New riding students learn by using the older horses.

It takes four to 10 years to learn dressage at the Spanish Riding School. Some of the best students later become teachers. That is how the knowledge of horsemanship is passed on.

It takes two to four more years to learn to train a young stallion. Only experienced riders are allowed to work with the young horses. Each rider works with only a couple of stallions. That way the horses and riders get to know and trust each other.

Dressage Training

A Lipizzaner stallion does not begin training until he is almost four. That is old compared to other horses. Many breeds are fully trained at two years old. A Lipizzaner stallion's training takes four years.

Young stallions leave the farm at Piber when they are three and one-half years old. Those chosen as Spanish Riding School horses go to Vienna. They live in a stable across the street from the Winter Riding Hall.

A stallion spends his first year in basic training. He learns how to take commands from the rider. He learns to move gracefully with a rider on his back. The horse and rider become like part of each other. These are the basics of dressage riding.

Lipizzaners learn controlled and graceful movements.

The next year is called the lower school or campaign school. The horse begins to learn gymnastic movements. These are designed to stretch his muscles. This makes the horse stronger and more athletic. His movements become more controlled and graceful.

Stallions that succeed in the lower school advance to the high school of dressage. This takes two more years of training. In the high school, horses learn more difficult movements.

Passage, Piaffe, and Pirouette

Three of these difficult movements are the passage, the piaffe, and the pirouette. The passage (puh-SAHJ) is like a floating trot. The horse holds one front foot and the opposite back foot in the air for a split second. The horse and rider look as if they are dancing on air.

In the piaffe (PEEYAHF), the horse prances in one spot. This is especially beautiful when performed to music. In the pirouette (peer-oh-WET), the horse stands on his hind legs and turns in a circle.

By the time a stallion masters the high school, he is between eight and 10 years old. He can do things few horses in the world ever learn. A handful of especially talented Lipizzaners go even further. They learn the battle leaps.

Airs Above the Ground

The battle leaps are called the "airs above the ground." These are the most difficult movements

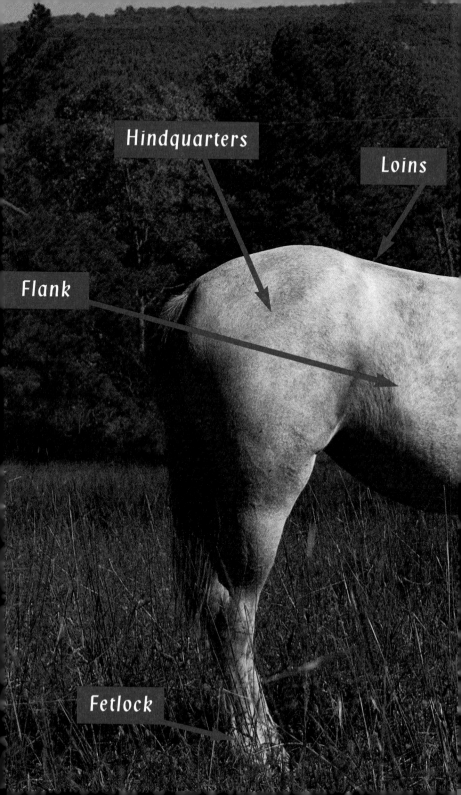

Hindquarters

Loins

Flank

Fetlock

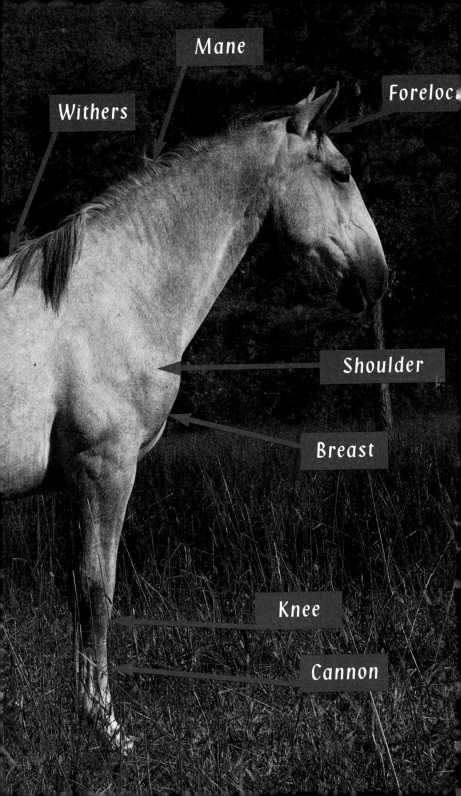

Mane

Forelock

Withers

Shoulder

Breast

Knee

Cannon

any horse has ever been taught to perform. They are called the levade, the courbette, the croupade, and the capriole. It takes years for a stallion to master them.

In ancient battles, the levade (luh-VAHD) allowed the soldier to see above the battle. To do the levade, the horse bends back on his hind legs. At the same time, he raises his front legs high in the air.

The courbette (kohr-BEHT) allowed a soldier to rush through an enemy line. To do the courbette, the horse holds his front legs in the air. Then he jumps forward on his hind legs.

The croupade (kroo-PAHD) was designed for quick escape from danger. To do the croupade, the horse leaps high into the air. All four feet are off the ground. He tucks his legs under him.

The capriole (kah-pree-OHL) is like the croupade except the horse kicks his back legs out behind him. This protects the rider from an enemy attack.

It takes years for a Lipizzaner to master the difficult movements they are taught.

Lipizzaners Today

Lipizzaners do not perform these leaps in battle anymore. But they are still thrilling to watch. People come to see the white stallions perform at the Spanish Riding School.

There are a few Lipizzaners that perform in shows in North America. Two groups are in Florida. One group performs year-round in Wadsworth, Illinois. Anther performs in Las Vegas, Nevada. Their shows are much like the ones at the Spanish Riding School.

There are not many farms in North America that raise Lipizzaners. But this is changing. More people are using Lipizzaners for dressage competitions. Others are finding that they make wonderful carriage horses.

People will always enjoy watching the beautiful white horses float across an arena. Lipizzaners give us a unique glimpse back in time. They are a link to the days when the world revolved around horses. It probably still does for those people who are fortunate enough to own a Lipizzaner.

Lipizzaners perform in traveling shows in North America.

Words to Know

capriole (kah-pree-OHL)—a leap in which the horse has all four feet off the ground, with the hind legs kicking out behind

courbette (kohr-BEHT)—a leap from the hind legs, with the horse holding the front legs in the air

croupade (kroo-PAHD)—a leap in which the horse has all four feet off the ground, with the legs tucked under

dressage (dreh-SAHJ)—a style of riding in which the horse performs complicated movements on command from the rider

foal (FOHL)—a young horse

horsemanship (HORSS-man-ship)—the ability to handle, use, and care for horses

levade (luh-VAHD)—a movement in which the horse balances on the hind legs

mare (MAIR)—a female horse

passage (puh-SAHJ)—a suspended, dancing trot

piaffe (PEEYAHF)—a movement in which the horse prances in one spot

pirouette (peer-oh-WET)—a movement in which the horse turns in a circle while balancing on its hind legs

stallion (STAL-yuhn)—a male horse

To Learn More

Edwards, Elwyn Hartley. *Encyclopedia of the Horse*. New York: Dorling Kindersley, 1994.

Henry, Marguerite. *White Stallion of Lipizza*. Chicago: Rand McNally & Company, 1964.

Micek, Tomas. *Lipizzaner Horses. Magnificent Horses of the World*. Milwaukee: Gareth Stevens, 1995.

Podhajsky, Alois. *The Lipizzaners*. New York: Doubleday, 1969.

Van der Linde, Laurel. *The White Stallions: The Story of the Dancing Horses of Lippizza*. New York: New Discovery Books, 1994.

You can read articles about Lipizzaner Horses in *Discover Horses, Equus, Horse and Horseman, Horse Illustrated, HorsePlay*, and *Lipizzan Journal*.

Useful Addresses

Canadian Horse Council
P.O. Box 156
Rexdale, ON M9W 5L2
Canada

Hermann's Lipizzan Ranch
32755 Singletary Road
Myakkia City, FL 34251

Lipizzan Association of North America
P.O. Box 1133
Anderson, IN 46015-1133
E-mail address: thull@iquest.net

Royal Lipizzaner Stallion Show
and **Loyal Lipizzan Fan Club**
1053 Van Arsdale Street
Oviedo, FL 32765
E-mail address: GaryL6988@aol.com

The Tempel Lipizzans
17000 Wadsworth Road
Wadsworth, IL 60083-9761

United States Dressage Federation
P.O. Box 6669
Lincoln, NE 68506-0669
E-mail address: jourkap@showme.missouri.edu

Internet Sites

Lipizzan Association of North America
http://www.astralite.com/WWW/lipizzan

Lipizzan Billboard
http://www.lipizzan.com

Royal Lipizzaner Stallion Show
http://www.lipizzaner.com

United States Dressage Federation
http://www.usdf.org

Index